MIGHTY MACHINES

Snowplows

by Mary Lindeen

BELLWETHER MEDIA • MINNEAPOLIS, MN

Note to Librarians, Teachers, and Parents:

Blastoff! Readers are carefully developed by literacy experts and combine standards-based content with developmentally-appropriate text.

Level 1 provides the most support through repetition of high-frequency words, light text, predictable sentence patterns, and strong visual support.

Level 2 offers early readers a bit more challenge through varied simple sentences, increased text load, and less repetition of high frequency words.

Level 3 advances early-fluent readers toward fluency through increased text and concept load, less reliance on visuals, longer sentences, and more literary language.

Level 4 builds reading stamina by providing more text per page, increased use of punctuation, greater variation in sentence patterns, and increasingly challenging vocabulary.

Level 5 encourages children to move from "learning to read" to "reading to learn" by providing even more text, varied writing styles, and less familiar topics.

Whichever book is right for your reader, Blastoff! Readers are the perfect books to build confidence and encourage a love of reading that will last a lifetime!

This edition first published in 2008 by Bellwether Media.

No part of this publication may be reproduced in whole or in part without written permission of the publisher. For information regarding permission, write to Bellwether Media Inc., Attention: Permissions Department, Post Office Box 1C, Minnetonka, MN 55345-9998.

Library of Congress Cataloging-in-Publication Data
Lindeen, Mary.
  Snowplows / by Mary Lindeen.
    p. cm. — (Mighty machines) (Blastoff! readers)
Summary: "Simple text and supportive images introduce young readers to Snowplows. Intended for students in kindergarten through third grade. "—Provided by publisher.
  Includes bibliographical references and index.
  ISBN-13: 978-1-60014-120-1 (hardcover : alk. paper)
  ISBN-10: 1-60014-120-X (hardcover : alk. paper)
  1. Snowplows–Juvenile literature. 2. Snow removal–Juvenile literature. I. Title.

TD868.L56 2008
625.10028'8–dc22
                                    2007009762

Text copyright © 2008 by Bellwether Media.
SCHOLASTIC, CHILDREN'S PRESS, and associated logos are trademarks and/or registered trademarks of Scholastic Inc. Printed in the United States of America.

Contents

A snowplow is
a big machine
that is used
in winter.

A snowplow has a **blade** in the front.

blade

The blade pushes snow off of the road. Then the road is clear for cars to drive.

MINNESOTA ET-5045 STATE VEHICLE

A snowplow has a **spreader**. This part sprays salt or sand onto the road.

spreader

Salt and sand make the road less slippery. Then cars can drive safely.

This truck has
a snowplow
on the front.
It clears
highways.

This box
snowplow
clears
parking lots.

This snowplow clears the sidewalk.

This airport snowplow clears **runways**. What a pile of snow!

Glossary

blade— the broad and flat part of a machine used to scrape and push things on the ground

highway—a large and important road

runway—a flat strip of land where airplanes take off and land

spreader—a machine used to scatter something on the ground

To Learn More

AT THE LIBRARY

Awdry, W. Rev. *Thomas Gets a Snowplow*.
New York: Random House, 2004

Randolph, Joanne. *Snowplows*. New York:
PowerKids Press, 2002.

Zuehlke, Jeffrey. *Snowplows*. Minneapolis,
Minn.: Lerner, 2006.

ON THE WEB

Learning more about mighty
machines is as easy as 1, 2, 3.

1. Go to www.factsurfer.com

2. Enter "mighty machines" into search box.

3. Click the "Surf" button and you will see a
   list of related web sites.

With factsurfer.com, finding more information
is just a click away.

Index

The photographs in this book are reproduced through the courtesy of: Adrian T. Jones, front cover; David R. Gonzalez/MNDOT, pp. 5, 7, 9, 11, 13; Raymond Forbes, p. 15; Esa Hitula/Alamy, p. 17; Robert Asento, p. 19; Michael Dywer/Alamy, p. 21.

7/09